SHORT WALKS
MADE EASY

CORNISH COAST

CW00763474

Ordnance Survey

Contents

Walk 1

BUDE

Distance
3 miles / 4.8 km

Time
2 hours   CATCH A BUS

Start/Finish
The Wharf, Bude

Parking EX23 8LG
Wharf long-stay car
park

Cafés/pubs
Bude

Low, grassy
clifftops with
Bude Bay views;
lovely canal
towpath

Page 14

Walk 2
TINTAGEL

Distance
1.5 miles/2.4km

Time
1 hour

CATCH A BUS

Start/Finish
Tintagel village

Parking PL34 0DD
Old Tintagel Country
Club car park

Cafés/pubs
Beach Café at Tintagel
Castle; Tintagel village

Dramatic,
atmospheric cliffs
and headlands; lure
of Arthurian myth

Page 20

Walk 3
PADSTOW

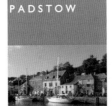

Distance
2.9 miles/4.6km

Time
2 hours

CATCH A BUS

Start/Finish
Padstow

Parking PL28 8BY
South Quay car park,
Riverside

Cafés/pubs
Padstow

The infamous
Doom Bar; fine
country house;
the 'Obby 'Oss
Festival

Page 28

Walk 4
ST AGNES

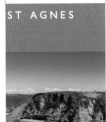

Distance
4.3 miles/6.9km

Time
2¾ hours

CATCH A BUS

Start/Finish
St Agnes

Parking TR5 0TP
Trelawny Road car
park

Cafés/pubs
St Agnes

Coastal heathland;
tin-mining
landscape World
Heritage Site

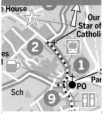

Page 34

Walk 5	Walk 6	Walk 7
ZENNOR	**HELSTON**	**THE LIZARD**

Distance
2.6 miles/4.1km

Time
1¾ hours

Start/Finish
Zennor

Parking TR26 3DA
Zennor car park

Cafés/pubs
Tinners Arms;
Moomaid ice cream
parlour

Artists and
writers; mermaid
legend; delicious
ice cream

Distance
3.2 miles/5.1km

Time
2 hours

Start/Finish
Helston

Parking TR13 0RA
Fairground car park,
Porthleven Road

Cafés/pubs
The Stables (NT);
Helston

Gentle, beautifully
wooded Loe
Valley walk on NT
Penrose Estate

Distance
2.7 miles/4.3km

Time
1¾ hours

Start/Finish
Lizard

Parking TR12 7NH
The Square car park

Cafés/pubs
Lizard village; Lizard
Point

Britain's most
southerly point;
lighthouse and
Cornish choughs

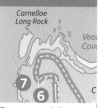

Page 42 Page 48 Page 54

Walk 8	Walk 9	Walk 10

TRELISSICK

Distance
3.1 miles/5km

Time
2 hours — CATCH A BUS

Start/Finish
Trelissick

Parking TR3 6QL
Trelissick National
Trust car park

Cafés/pubs
Crofters Café (NT),
Trelissick

Lush woodland
beside creek and
riverside; NT
gardens; River Fal
ferry

LOST GARDENS OF HELIGAN

Distance
3.9 miles/6.2km

Time
2½ hours — CATCH A BUS

Start/Finish
Mevagissey

Parking PL26 6SB
Willow car and coach
park, Valley Road

Cafés/pubs
Lost Gardens of
Heligan; Mevagissey

Magical sub-
tropical gardens;
historic fishing
village; easy
walking

MOUNT EDGCUMBE

Distance
2.2 miles/3.6km

Time
1½ hours — TAKE A FERRY

Start/Finish
Mount Edgcumbe

Parking PL1 3RL,
Plymouth (for Cremyll
Ferry); PL10 1HU,
Cremyll car park

Cafés/pubs
The Farriers and
The Orangery cafés;
Edgcumbe Arms

Ferry ride across
The Sound;
country park,
gardens and cafés

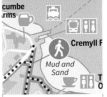

GETTING OUTSIDE ON THE CORNISH COAST

> **"** be enchanted by the romantic mystery of a mermaid's tale at St Senara's

OS Champion
Fi Darby

Merlin's Cave, Tintagel

A very warm welcome to the new Short Walks Made Easy guide to the Cornish Coast – what a fantastic selection of leisurely walks we have for you!

The most south-westerly county of England, Cornwall occupies a tapering peninsula pushing into the North Atlantic. It has more than 300 miles of stunning coastline, much of it falling into the 11 constituent parts comprising (with Bodmin Moor) the Cornwall Area of Outstanding Natural Beauty, designated back in 1959, and covering 370 square miles or almost one-third of the county.

Set amid gorgeous scenery, these ten superb coastal walks explore the incredible diversity of the Cornish coast: dramatically wild and rugged cliffs and coves at Tintagel and The Lizard; lushly wooded valleys along the sinuous shores to Helston and Trelissick; and exotic subtropical gardens at Heligan and Mount Edgcumbe. You can follow in the footsteps of artists and writers at Zennor; tour the remarkable tin-mining heritage around St Agnes; and enjoy a café stop perched high above the British mainland's most southerly point, as well as a post-walk seafood dinner at Padstow. There's the chance to be impressed by Georgian engineering while strolling beside the Bude Canal, to be enchanted by the romantic mystery of a mermaid's tale at St Senara's Church, and to be tempted by a delicious Cornish ice cream after every walk.

Fi Darby, OS Champion

WE SMILE MORE
WHEN WE'RE OUTSIDE

Polpeor Cove, The Lizard

Whether it's a short walk during our lunch break or a full day's outdoor adventure, we know that a good dose of fresh air is just the tonic we all need.

At Ordnance Survey (OS), we're passionate about helping more people to get outside more often. It sits at the heart of everything we do, and through our products and services, we aim to help you lead an active outdoor lifestyle, so that you can live longer, stay younger and enjoy life more.

We firmly believe the outdoors is for everyone, and we want to help you find the very best Great Britain has to offer. We are blessed with an island that is beautiful and unique, with a rich and varied landscape. There are coastal paths to meander along, woodlands to explore, countryside to roam, and cities to uncover. Our trusted source of inspirational content is bursting with ideas for places to go, things to do and easy beginner's guides on how to get started.

It can be daunting when you're new to something, so we want to bring you the know-how from the people who live and breathe the outdoors. To help guide us, our team of awe-inspiring OS Champions share their favourite places to visit, hints and tips for outdoor adventures, as well as tried and tested accessible, family- and wheelchair-friendly routes. We hope that you will feel inspired to spend more time outside and reap the physical and mental health benefits that the outdoors has to offer. With our handy guides, paper and digital mapping, and exciting new apps, we can be with you every step of the way.

To find out more visit os.uk/getoutside

RESPECTING
THE COUNTRYSIDE

You can't beat getting outside in the British countryside, but it's vital that we leave no trace when we're enjoying the great outdoors.

Let's make sure that generations to come can enjoy the countryside just as we do.

 Leave no trace

 Keep dogs under control; bin and bag waste

 Do not light fires; only BBQ at official sites

 Leave gates as you find them

 Keep to footpaths and open access land

 Plan ahead for your trip

For more details please visit
www.gov.uk/countryside-code

USING THIS GUIDE

Easy-to-follow Cornish Coast walks for all

Before setting off
Check the walk information panel to plan your outing
- Consider using **Public transport** where flagged. If driving, note the satnav postcode for the car park under **Parking**
- The suggested **Time** is based on a gentle pace
- Note the availability of **Cafés**, tearooms and pubs, and **Toilets**

Terrain and hilliness
- **Terrain** indicates the nature of the route surface
- Any rises and falls are noted under **Hilliness**

Walking with your dog?
- This panel states where **Dogs** must be on a lead and how many stiles there are – in case you need to lift your dog
- Keep dogs on leads where there are livestock and between April and August in forest and on grassland where there are ground-nesting birds

A perfectly pocket-sized walking guide
- Handily sized for ease of use on each walk
- When not being read, it fits nicely into a pocket...
- ...so between points, put this book in the pocket of your coat, trousers or day sack and enjoy your stroll in glorious countryside – we've made it pocket-sized for a reason!

Flexibility of route presentation to suit all readers
- **Not comfortable map reading?** Then use the simple-to-follow route profile and accompanying route description and pictures
- **Happy to map read?** New-look walk mapping makes it easier for you to focus on the route and the points of interest along the way
- **Read the insightful Did you know?, Local legend, Stories behind the walk** and **Nature notes** to help you make the most of your day out and to enjoy all that each walk has to offer

OS information about the walk

• Many of the features and symbols shown are taken from Ordnance Survey's celebrated **Explorer** mapping, designed to help people across Great Britain enjoy leisure time spent outside

• National Grid reference for the start point

• Explorer sheet map covering the route

The easy-to-use walk map

• **Large-scale** mapping for ultra-clear route finding

• **Numbered points** at key turns along the route that tie in with the route instructions and respective points marked on the profile

• **Pictorial symbols** for intuitive map reading, see Map Symbols on the front cover flap

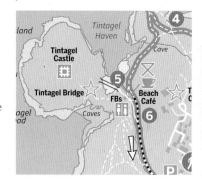

The simple-to-follow walk profile

• Progress easily along the route using the illustrative profile, it has **numbered points** for key turning points and **graduated distance** markers

• Easy-read **route directions** with turn-by-turn detail

• Reassuring **route photographs** for each numbered point

🔵 South West Coast Path

Tintagel Haven (right) · **Tintagel Castle** (right)

1 mile
Beach Café

5 ➤ At the café and picnic tables, turn **left** to pass the shop and toilets to reach the gravel access track.

Using QR codes

- Scan each QR code to see the route in Ordnance Survey's OS Maps App.
NB You may need to download a scanning app if you have an older phone

- OS Maps will open the route automatically if you have it installed. If not, the route will open in the web version of OS Maps

- Please click **Start Route** button to begin navigating or **Download Route** to store the route for offline use

WALK 1

BUDE

Bude is a curious anomaly: ostensibly a pleasant little seaside resort, it's not quite on the seaside. The vast majority of the town rather lies behind the River Neet and the Bude Canal, leaving the nearby coastline satisfyingly untamed. This walk heads speedily out of town to roam the low grassy clifftops. The return is made along the picturesque Bude Canal, an impressive feat of late Georgian engineering, whose ingenious method of raising and lowering boats makes it almost unique in Britain.

CATCH A BUS

OS information
SS 206 062 Explorer 111
Distance 3 miles/4.8 km
Time 2 hours
Start/Finish The Wharf, Bude
Parking EX23 8LG Wharf long-stay car park, The Wharf
Public toilets The Crescent long-stay car park, near finish, 225 yards south-east of The Wharf
Cafés/pubs Bude
Terrain Lanes; grassy and tarmac paths
Hilliness Two gentle ascents and one descent on the coast path 3 to 5
Footwear Year round

Public transport

Bus services link Bude with Barnstaple, Okehampton, Plymouth, Launceston, Holsworthy and Newquay: stagecoachbus.com; gocornwallbus.co.uk

Accessibility

Wheelchair and pushchair friendly from **6** and along the Bude Canal towpath

Dogs

Welcome. No stiles

Did you know? In 1838, the Bude Light was invented by Sir Goldsworthy Gurney. By injecting oxygen into an oil flame he produced a light 2.5 times brighter than an ordinary oil lamp. It so impressed eminent scientist Sir Michael Faraday that he recommended its use in lighthouses. Sadly, it proved too expensive, but it was used to illuminate the Houses of Parliament, Trafalgar Square and Pall Mall, as well as Gurney's home, The Castle (see page 16).

Local legend Bude is home to a rather unlikely legend – or rather, a structure that has become legendary. In 2018, a jokey review of the 76-yard perspex tunnel beside the town's Sainsbury's went viral, propelling it into the national news. There is actually something rather impressive about the tunnel's 36 arches and arrow-straight design, particularly when adorned with Christmas lights. Its popularity continues today, with visitors coming from far and wide to see it.

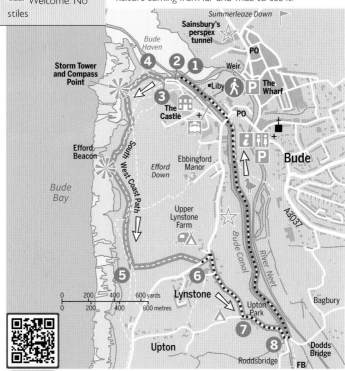

Scan Me

STORIES BEHIND THE WALK

🏠 **The Castle** According to the parable, it's a fool who builds their house upon the sands. That didn't deter inventor Sir Goldsworthy Gurney. In 1830, this forgotten genius devised a way of building The Castle among the dunes at Bude. His contemporaries scornfully warned him it would collapse, but time has proved them wrong. The building has served as a luxurious home, council offices, magistrate's court and library, but now hosts an excellent heritage centre (thecastlebude.co.uk).

☆ **Bude Canal** Completed in 1823 to transport lime-rich sand for use as fertiliser, this is one of Britain's most unusual canals. Although it rose 433 feet from its sea-level starting point, its 35-mile network boasted just two conventional locks. Instead, wheeled boats were raised or lowered on inclined planes between differing levels of water by a system of chains powered by waterwheels. The 5 miles that remain today are in the care of the Bude Canal Trust.

The Castle (right)
Bude Canal ☆ Sea lock
The Wharf
Steps
Steps
South West Coast Path
Bude Haven (right)
Storm Tower and Compass Point
✳ ½ mile

🅿 Wharf long-stay car park

➡ Leave the car park at The Wharf Craft Shops and Old Forge sign and walk alongside the canal (on your left) towards the sea to reach the sea lock.

① ➡ **Cross** the canal via the sea lock gates. Turn **right** on the other side along a lane for 20 yards to a flight of steps.

☀ Storm Tower and Compass Point

Shortly after reaching the coast, you'll pass a curious octagonal building called the Storm Tower. Designed by George Wightwick for Sir Thomas Dyke Acland in 1835, it bears points of the compass on its eight faces. The tower is reputed to have been inspired by the Tower of the Winds in Athens, which would be appropriate given its blustery location. Though certainly ornamental, its purpose is unclear, but it may have been intended as a shelter for local coastguards.

☆ Gorsedh Kernow

Literally meaning 'Cornish Throne', Gorsedh Kernow is both an organisation and annual event dedicated to preserving Cornwall's Celtic spirit. It was founded in 1928 by Henry Jenner to help revive the lost Cornish language. The festive gathering has occurred annually ever since (save during World War II), with men and women anointed as bards for their services to the Cornish tongue. Bude has had the honour of hosting the Gorsedh three times: in 1961, 1975 and 2021.

Efford Beacon | Efford Down | **5** | **6**

1 mile

2 ➡ Climb the steps to your **left** and continue **right** along a road to its end.

3 ➡ At the end, climb the steps and turn **right** at a South West Coast Path fingerpost.
➡ Walk 175 yards to a fork.

NATURE NOTES

Rather rarely for Britain, this walk takes in both a canal and a rocky coastline. The former attracts birds like the familiar mallard and Canada goose, both of which enjoy the shelter and placid waters on offer. The shoreline is the domain of waders such as the oystercatcher, instantly recognisable by its dramatic black and white wing markings and its long orange bill made for prising open shellfish, as its name suggests.

Often seen in both locations are black-headed gulls, whose chocolate-brown (not black) heads turn white in winter aside from a dark spot on each side.

Blackthorn, whose fruit is used to make sloe gin, can be found growing inland, along with hemp agrimony, once valued for its anti-inflammatory properties.

In spring, bright yellow lesser celandines create splashes of colour in the hedgerows alongside the canal towpath.

Sloes

Lynstone

1½ miles

☆ Bude Canal

2 miles

4 ➡ Take the unwaymarked grassy path to the **left** leading uphill to the tower on Compass Point.
➡ Go through a kissing-gate 300 yards beyond the tower.
➡ Stay on the coast path for ½ mile to a gate at the top of a rise.

5 ➡ At the gate, turn **left** along the field edge (hedge on right).
➡ This path leads through a kissing-gate. Head onwards, now with a hedge to your left, soon going downwards to a road on your right.

6 ➡ Turn **left** along the pavement and after 100 yards cross the road and turn **right** down a lane for ¼ mile to a junction.

Above: oystercatcher
Below: lesser celandine

Top: black-headed gull
Above: Canada goose
Below: mallard

☆ Bude Canal

3 miles
The Wharf

2½ miles

The Crescent
long-stay car park

ℹ️ 🅿️ 🚻

Wharf
long-stay car park

🅿️

8 ➡ **Cross** the bridge over the canal and immediately turn **left** through a gate and onto the metalled towpath.
➡ Continue for 1 mile beside the canal back to the car park, crossing a road along the way.

7 ➡ At the T-junction turn **left** along the lane for 350 yards to reach the Bude Canal.

TINTAGEL

Very nearly an island and seemingly intent on breaking off from the mainland altogether, Tintagel Head is one of the most romantic and mystical locations in Britain. This walk heads out from the eponymous village to explore a little of the rugged coastline before arriving at the castle itself. Along the way it takes in Barras Nose, a small headland that provides both the very best views of the castle and a great spot for a picnic.

OS information		
🚶 SX 055886 Explorer 111		
Distance 1.5 miles/2.4 km		
Time 1 hour		
Start/Finish Tintagel village		
Parking PL34 0DD Old Tintagel Country Club car park, Atlantic Road		
Public toilets Tintagel Castle; Tintagel Visitor Centre		
Cafés/pubs The Beach Café at Tintagel Castle; Tintagel village		
Terrain Lanes and tarmac paths; gravel tracks; grassy paths		
Hilliness One moderate climb towards the end		
Footwear Spring/Autumn/ Winter 👟 Summer 👟		

Did you know? Tintagel Castle has helped dispel a long-standing but mistaken belief about the Dark Ages. In 2016–17, digs carried out by Cornwall Archaeological Unit revealed the existence of a palace from around the 6th century. What proved even more important was the discovery of slate with writing on it. At a stroke, all those history books proclaiming that everyone in Dark Ages Britain was illiterate would have to be re-written.

Local legend The popularity of the myth of King Arthur is largely down to one man: the prolific 12th-century writer Geoffrey of Monmouth. In his *History of the Kings of Britain*, he chose to have King Arthur conceived at Tintagel with some magical help from Merlin. Today, Arthur's rich legend encompasses the Knights of the Round Table, the quest for the Holy Grail, the Lady of the Lake and, of course, the pulling of the sword from the stone.

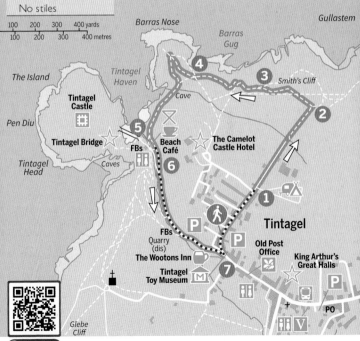

STORIES BEHIND THE WALK

☆ **Tintagel Bridge** August 2019 saw the opening of a bridge between the mainland and the castle, finally replacing the narrow natural land-bridge lost sometime in the Middle Ages. Some observers opposed the crossing, calling it a desecration of the historic site. However, the elegant cantilever bridge – designed to evoke Arthur's sword Excalibur – appears to have few critics today. Rather thrillingly, its two sides don't quite meet in the middle – there's a small gap between them.

⊞ Tintagel Castle

Tintagel's precipitous and easily defensible slopes created a highly desirable stronghold for many centuries. Rulers of Cornwall made it their citadel and Richard, Earl of Cornwall, built himself a castle here in the 1230s, apparently inspired by the myths already surrounding the site. However, its location was of no strategic value at all and the castle fell into ruin soon after Richard died, adding further romance to the headland.

Atlantic Road   ☆ **The Camelot Castle Hotel** (left)

🅿 Old Tintagel Country Club car park

Headland Caravan Park

➼ Leave the car park by the vehicle entrance/exit and turn **right** along Atlantic Road.
➼ When the pavement changes sides, **cross** the road to continue to a sharp left bend.

① ➼ At the bend, carry **straight on** past the Headland Caravan Park along a rutted track.
➼ At a gate into a field, go **straight ahead** beside a hedge/wall, following a Coast Path sign to a gate at the field end.

☆ Thomas Hardy

It's perhaps a little surprising that an author so strongly associated with Dorset should feature in a book of Cornish walks. However, Hardy was a frequent visitor to Tintagel and was so taken by the castle that he wrote a one-act play set here. *The Famous Tragedy of the Queen of Cornwall at Tintagel in Lyonnesse* was published in 1923 and is based on the legend of Tristan and Iseult.

☆ The Camelot Castle Hotel

No visitor to Tintagel can fail to notice the lone castle-like building on a clifftop mound nearby. Built in 1896 and originally named King Arthur's Castle Hotel, it was intended to cater for tourists arriving by train. Unfortunately, the proposed railway never materialised. The hotel includes a Romanesque Great Hall, designed to look like the Winchester Round Table, and offers guests an Arthurian experience with fantastic coastal vistas, to mixed reviews.

½ mile

 3

⚑ **South West Coast Path**

Barras Nos

4

2 ➥ Pass through the gate and turn **left** onto a path.
➥ A brief descent will bring you to a T-junction.

3 ➥ Turn **left** and head along the coast.
➥ At a gate, continue forwards, passing a National Trust Barras Nose sign, to reach a junction giving onto the headland.

NATURE NOTES

The coastline around Tintagel is composed of Old Devonian slate. The two rocky headlands on this walk – Tintagel Head and Barras Nose – are sea-formed features, and the natural protection offered by both may well have seen them used as defensive sites as far back as the Mesolithic period (10,000–6,000 years ago).

Although the dramatic scenery may seem austere and even barren, you'll find the globular pink heads of thrift and the more vibrant pink sorrel growing here. Look out too for sea lavender. It's not a relative of lavender but probably owes its name to its delicate lavender-hued flowers. Two other plants that may take a little more patience to seek out are wild thyme, which thrives on thin

soils and rocky outcrops, and sea plantain, with its distinctive rosette finger-like leaves, the shape of which also gives rise to its other common name, goose tongue.

Autumn squill carpets the grassy slopes and clifftop pathways from July to September and, at the same time of year, watch out for the grayling butterfly. Although nationally uncommon, it tends to frequent rocky outcrops and warmer bare ground, where its colouration makes it incredibly well camouflaged.

Tintagel Haven (right)   **Tintagel Castle** (right)

1 mile

Beach Café

4 ➡ Go **right** for an anti-clockwise circuit of Barras Nose headland.
➡ The circuit concludes with some steps downhill. When you reach the foot, turn **right** to continue along the coast path for 350 yards to the Beach Café.

5 ➡ At the café and picnic tables, turn **left** to pass the shop and toilets to reach the gravel access track.

Top left: grayling butterfly
Above: sea plantain
Top right: autumn squill
Opposite: thrift

Pink sorrel

Castle Road

The Wootons Inn; Tintagel Toy Museum

Atlantic Road
1½ miles

Old Tintagel Country Club car park

6 ➡ A wide track (Castle Road) leads all the way up to the village.
➡ To visit the castle, turn **right** after 250 yards to go up the slope to the ticket office. Otherwise, continue to the top of the track.

7 ➡ When you emerge beside The Wootons Inn and Tintagel Toy Museum, turn **left** along Atlantic Road to return to the car park.

This page (clockwise): Bude Canal; old lifeboat station, Polpeor Cove; Zennor church; The Lizard
Opposite (clockwise): Barras Nose; St Agnes Beacon; Cremyll Ferry, Mount Edgcumbe

Cremyll Ferry Timetable
(WINTER SERVICE)

QUEUE HERE FOR CREMYLL FERRY

THANKYOU

WEEKDAY	SATURDAY
06.45	7.30 8.00
07.30	8.30
08.15	Then on the hour
09.00	and half past the
09.30	hour.
	Last Ferry 18.00
Then on the hour	
and half past the	
hour.	
Last Ferry 18.30	

WALK 3

CATCH A BUS

PADSTOW

Famous for its fine dining and picturesque harbour, Padstow has evolved over the centuries from a vital safe haven on the rocky north coast to a fishing port and a popular tourist destination. This walk starts right by the harbour where you may still see a few fishing boats among the yachts and pleasure craft. The stroll along the Camel estuary takes in the Doom Bar sand bank and a World War II battery before heading back over farmland to Elizabethan Prideaux Place.

OS information

🚶 SW 920753
Explorer 106

Distance
2.9 miles/4.6 km

Time
2 hours

Start/Finish
Padstow

Parking PL28 8BY
South Quay car park,
Riverside

Public toilets
North Quay, ❶

Cafés/pubs
Padstow

Terrain
Lane, pavement and tarmac path; tracks and grassy paths

Hilliness
A short climb to St Saviour's Point ❷ and subsequent descent; a longer but moderate ascent after ❹ and descent to Prideaux Place ❺

Footwear
Winter 🥾
Spring/Summer/
Autumn 👟

Public transport
Bus services from Plymouth via Liskeard, Bodmin and Wadebridge, and from Newquay via Wadebridge: gocornwallbus.co.uk

Did you know? Padstow and Bodmin may be 11 miles apart and found in very different settings, but they were intimately linked during the Middle Ages. After a Viking raid in 981, the monks of Saint Petroc's monastery moved from Padstow (then named Petroc-stow) up to the relative safety of the moor. For centuries afterwards, Padstow was known as Aldestowe ('old place') while the monks' new home was called Bodmin ('new place').

Local legend The 400-year-old Prideaux Place (see page 31) is said to host a number of spectres. The most frequently seen is that of a small boy who races around the kitchen. Goings-on in the Grenville Room sound rather less pleasant: tales are of a phantom red-eyed dog snarling and scaring visitors away. Meanwhile the staircase and landing are the preserve of various ghostly women in an assortment of coloured outfits.

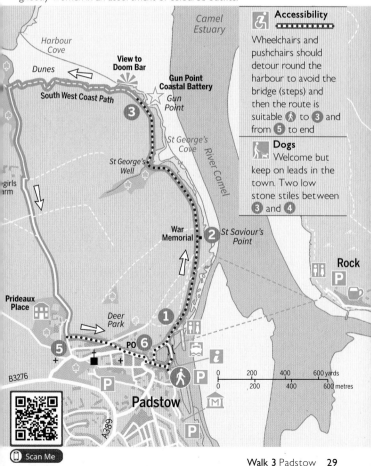

Accessibility
Wheelchairs and pushchairs should detour round the harbour to avoid the bridge (steps) and then the route is suitable 🚶 to ③ and from ⑤ to end

Dogs
Welcome but keep on leads in the town. Two low stone stiles between ③ and ④

Camel Estuary

Harbour Cove

Dunes

View to Doom Bar

Gun Point Coastal Battery
Gun Point

South West Coast Path

③

St George's Cove

River Camel

St George's Well

-girls arm

War Memorial

② St Saviour's Point

Rock

Prideaux Place

Deer Park

①

⑤

PO ⑥

B3276

Padstow

A389

0   200   400   600 yards
0   200   400   600 metres

STORIES BEHIND THE WALK

⚡ **Doom Bar** Made famous by the beer to which it gives its name, Doom Bar has been the nemesis of many a hapless sailor. A sandbar at the mouth of the Camel estuary, it's formed of sediment pushed up by the incoming tide. Over 600 wrecks, strandings and capsizes have been recorded here since the early 19th century. *HMS Whiting* is the bar's only warship casualty, foundering here in 1816. While no one drowned, three deserting crewmen each received 50 lashes.

☆ **Gun Point Coastal Battery**

Lying on the route of the walk near the dunes of Harbour Cove, this coastal battery was erected hastily in the summer of 1940 amid fears of a German invasion. It was one of the northernmost defences of a 'stop line' that ran across Bodmin Moor to Fowey on the south coast. It was built on a battery established during the American War of Independence to guard against privateers such as John Paul Jones.

Padstow harbour

½ mile

War memorial; St Saviour's Point

R i v e

South Quay car park

➡ Leave the car park via the metal footbridge over the harbour entrance (wheelchair and pushchair users should head **clockwise** round the harbour).
➡ Continue to the road, cross it and turn **right**, walking 50 yards to the toilet block.

1 ➡ By the toilets, bear **left** up a slope on a tarmac path signed Lower Beach.
➡ Continue along the path to reach a Celtic cross war memorial.

☆ **'Obby 'Oss Festival** Unique to Padstow, the 'Obby 'Oss Festival takes place every May Day. Though its origins are obscure, the folk festival is known to be over 200 years old. Townsfolk dressed in white with coloured scarves parade in two separate processions singing and playing accordions, melodeons and drums. Each has its 'Obby 'Oss – an extravagant hobby-horse costume worn by one of the male dancers beneath which he tries to trap unsuspecting young women.

🏛 Prideaux Place

Built in 1592 by lawyer Sir Nicholas Prideaux, this fine Elizabethan manor house has been the seat of the Prideaux family ever since. Lording it above the port of Padstow, it has seen much but changed little in the intervening four centuries. Winston Graham, author of the popular *Poldark* series, was a frequent visitor here so it's fitting that scenes from the 2015 television adaptation were filmed on the estate (prideauxplace. co.uk).

George's Cove | **Gun Point Coastal Battery** ☆ | dunes | **View to Doom Bar** ☆ | 🔺 **South West Coast Path**

amel | 1 mile | dunes

2 ➡ Pass through a wide gate beside a stone stile and head **straight on**. Keep on the South West Coast Path, ignoring paths off.
➡ After winding round St George's Cove, continue for another 350 yards to Gun Point.

3 ➡ At the remains of the Gun Point Coastal Battery continue onwards, crossing two low stone stiles.
➡ The dunes make an excellent picnic spot in fine weather, with Doom Bar lying off them.
➡ Continue to a path T-junction.

NATURE NOTES

Padstow enjoys an enviably sheltered position on the Camel estuary. The path along the west bank is garlanded with flora, making full use of the protection from the worst of the Atlantic gales. The cheerful yellows of toadflax mix with the bold pink of valerian, the dusky tones of old man's beard (also called traveller's joy) when setting seed, and the brilliant white of yarrow. The evergreen hart's-tongue fern is identifiable by its rosette of long bright green fronds with undulated edges.

On the path above the dunes west of Gun Point, ③ to ④, look out for the white-lipped snail, a mollusc often found on dunes. Its favourite foods are common nettle and ragwort and, like crustaceans, it can form substantial colonies.

The fallow deer herd at Prideaux Place live in what is believed to be one of the oldest deer parks in the country, the land first becoming enclosed for this purpose in late Roman times.

White-lipped snails

Tregirls Farm

2 miles

Harbour Cove ¦ 1½ miles

④

dunes

④ ➤ Turn **left** to leave the coast path up a track. It becomes a metalled lane after Tregirls Farm.

➤ After ½ mile, pass through a stone arch to reach Prideaux Place. Look out for fallow deer in the parkland (left).

⑤ ➤ Almost immediately after Prideaux Place, turn **left** by The Dower House down Fentonluna Lane.

➤ Continue **ahead** as the road changes its name to Cross Street then Duke Street and keep **forward** to reach Market Place.

Fallow deer

Top left:
hart's-tongue fern
Top middle: valerian
Top right: old man's beard
Above: toadflax

Prideaux Place

Deer park
(left)

5

2½ miles

6

South Quay
car park

P

6 ⇒ At Market Place, carry
straight on along the
pedestrianised Market Strand.
⇒ When you reach the
harbour you can pass round
either side to return to
the car park.

Gun Point Coastal Battery

CATCH A BUS

ST AGNES

There's something authentically Cornish about St Agnes, from the Victorian splendour of the Miners and Mechanics Institute to the timeless solidity of the St Agnes Hotel. You cannot spend long here without noticing the outline of a tall chimney or an engine house, for this was once mining country. You'll pass both on this walk along a bracing stretch of north Cornish cliffs, while also visiting a coastal lookout station and a lonely sentry box with a story to tell.

OS information	
🏃 SW 719504 Explorer 104	
Distance 4.3 miles / 6.9 km	
Time 2¾ hours	
Start/Finish St Agnes	
Parking TR5 0TP Trelawny Road car park	
Public toilets Churchtown, St Agnes (close to ❶ and ❾); just off route at Trevaunance Cove	
Cafés/pubs St Agnes	
Terrain Pavement, lane, tracks, rocky footpaths, grassy clifftop paths	

🔲 Scan Me

Local legend Each year, on the Sunday before May Day, the residents of St Agnes re-enact the legend of Bolster the giant. Though married, the colossus fell in love with the young and beautiful Agnes and pursued her. After several local men had lost duels with him, Agnes cannily declared that Bolster should prove his love by filling a hole in a cliff with his blood. He duly died in the attempt. There's a moral there somewhere.

Hilliness
Descent and ascent near Trevaunance Cove ② to ④; gentler climb and descent at St Agnes Beacon

Footwear
Year round 👢

Public transport
Bus services 315, between Redruth and St Agnes, and U1A, between Truro and Newquay: hopleyscoaches.com and firstbus.co.uk/cornwall

Accessibility ♿
On sections in St Agnes only for wheelchairs and pushchairs, 🚶 to ②, and ⑨ to end

Dogs
Welcome but keep on leads in St Agnes. Five step-stiles

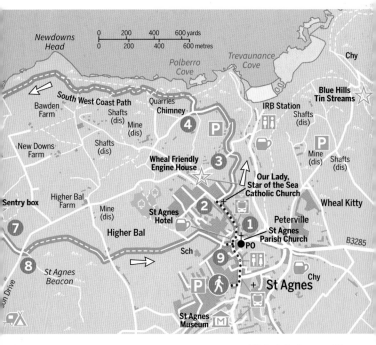

STORIES BEHIND THE WALK

☆ **Tin mining** Part of UNESCO's Cornwall and West Devon Mining Landscape World Heritage Site, St Agnes was once an important centre for tin extraction. At its peak, Wheal Coates mine employed 140 workers and was active for most of the 19th century until the tin price collapsed. However, the St Agnes tin story isn't over. Gathering tin ore from the coastline, Blue Hills Tin Streams (cornishtin. com) has been producing tin for nearly 50 years, making it unique in Britain.

☆ **Cameron Camp**
A lone breeze block sentry box **7** bears a plaque declaring that it was once part of Cameron Camp. Built on the clifftops in 1939, the camp initially served as a training post for the 10th Light Anti-Aircraft Battery. Later, thousands of Allied troops passed through here prior to D-Day. Though once covering a substantial area and boasting its own theatre, today only the sentry box remains.

St Agnes Museum
(300 yards, right)

St Agnes Parish Church

Our Lady, Star of the Sea Catholic Church

½ mile ☆

Trevaunance Cove (400 yards, right)

Chim...

St Agnes Hotel

Wheal Friendly Engine House

1 m...

Trelawny Road car park

➤ Turn **right** out of car park entrance then **left** at the road T-junction.
➤ Continue along Vicarage Road, ignoring turnings to the right, until you reach St Agnes Parish Church at the top of Town Hill.

1 ➤ Opposite the church, turn **left** up Trevaunance Road, walking 300 yards to Our Lady, Star of the Sea Catholic Church at a road junction.

2 ➤ Turn **right** along Wheal Friendly Lane.
➤ After the former engine house, the track becomes an uneven footpath with steps downhill. Ignore a crossing path and when you come to a broad track, turn **left** for 30 yards to meet a lane.

☆ Wheal Friendly Engine House

Completed in 1902, the engine house after ②
contained powerful pumping equipment. The Wheal

Friendly mine was extensive – joining up underground with Wheal Kitty on the other side of the valley – and keeping it dry was a constant challenge. The mine closed in 1930 and the engine house was left to moulder for nearly 90 years before restoration work began. It now incorporates a private house designed to give an impression of the boiler house that once stood here.

☆ St Agnes Museum

The village of St Agnes may have a population of just 2,000 but it has an excellent museum. Not content with displaying the sort of local artefacts and information you might expect to find, it also has exhibitions on local mining, maritime history, farming, folklore, Victoriana and much more besides. You can even buy a little ingot of St Agnes tin (stagnesmuseum.org.uk).

Polberro Cove — South West Coast Path — 1½ miles — Newdowns Head — 2 miles

③ ➡ **Cross** the lane onto a public footpath beside Little Orchard Cottage.
➡ Follow it to the top, where the path turns sharp **right** and becomes a metalled lane.
➡ Follow the lane for 350 yards to a tall chimney.

④ ➡ Turn **right** onto a track. In 150 yards go **left** to join the South West Coast Path.
➡ Follow coast path for 1½ miles to St Agnes Head (NCI lookout station, left).
➡ Rounding headland, about 350 yards after NCI station, reach a prominent post.

NATURE NOTES

There was a time when this part of Cornwall was dominated by an enormous expanse of heathland. Sadly, the area explored by this walk – St Agnes Beacon and the nearby clifftops – is now one of just a handful of isolated fragments that remain of this increasingly rare habitat. Towards the end of summer, you'll see it at its most colourful, when heather and gorse combine to give the landscape a luscious purple and yellow coat.

A nationally designated protected area, the St Agnes Heritage Coast is scattered with reminders of its mining past, now left to the mercies of seabirds such as the great black-backed gull. This is Britain's largest gull, with a heavy yellow bill and (in a fully grown adult) a black back and upper wings. It is noticeably bigger and bulkier than its more common cousin the herring gull, which has lighter grey upper parts and black wing tips.

Top: heather
Above: small heath

St Agnes Head
(NCI lookout station (left)

Cameron Camp ☆
(sentry box)

St Agr
Beacc

3 miles

South West Coast Path

2½ miles

⑤ ➡ At the post, near a left-hand bend in the clifftop-hugging path, turn **left** off the coast path up to a small car park.

⑥ ➡ At car park, pass a boulder (right) bearing a memorial plaque and turn immediately **left**.
➡ Ignoring side paths, keep **forward** for ⅓ mile to a step-stile, after which path becomes a metalled road and leads out to a lane junction.

⑦ ➡ At T-junction, go **right** along road, passing a sentry box – all that is left of Cameron Camp (see page 36).
➡ The road ends at another T-junction.

On St Agnes Beacon, you may meet the resident magpies or see a small heath, an attractive orange and fawn butterfly that flies only in sunshine and always perches with wings closed.

Above: herring gull
Below: magpie

Heathland

3½ miles

4 miles

St Agnes Museum
(300 yards, ahead) 🏛

9

Beaconsfield Place

Trelawny Road car park

8 ➧ **Cross** over and take footpath to **left** of National Trust sign.
➧ Ignore an upward path on right, and go on to cross a road then keep **ahead** on field paths over four step-stiles.
➧ The path becomes a rutted lane to reach Beaconsfield Place.

9 ➧ **Cross** over Beaconsfield Place to go along an alleyway. This brings you back to St Agnes Parish Church **1**.
➧ Turn **right** to retrace your steps to the start.

Opposite (clockwise): sea campion;
fallow deer; great crested grebe
This page (clockwise): orange pore
fungus; Lost Gardens of Heligan;
Camellia sasanqua (Hugh Evans);
basking shark

WALK 5

CATCH A BUS

ZENNOR

Aside from a short-lived population explosion during the 19th-century mining boom, for most of its long life Zennor has been little more than a hamlet. Yet its rich history is filled with household names: DH Lawrence, Virginia Woolf, Michael Morpurgo, Patrick Heron, even Emperor Haile Selassie. It also boasts a pub built in 1271. This route begins and ends in the village, crossing its tiny fields and taking a ramble out onto its rugged and lonely coast.

OS information

SW 454384
Explorer 102

Distance
2.6 miles/4.1km

Time
1¾ hours

Start/Finish
Zennor

Parking TR26 3DA
Zennor car park

Public toilets
None (for customers at the Tinners Arms)

Cafés/pubs
Tinners Arms and Moomaid ice cream parlour in village

Terrain
Lanes, tracks, clifftop and grassy paths

Hilliness
One climb, from **8** to **9**

Footwear
Year round

 Public transport
Bus stop 300 yards east of village on B3306. Bus service 16A linking Zennor with Penzance and St Ives:
gocornwallbus.co.uk

Did you know? In 1956, the renowned artist Patrick Heron moved into a house called Eagle's Nest on the cliffs near Zennor. He was in his mid-30s at the time and the move brought about one of the most productive periods of his career. Heron lived in the house until his death in 1999. Many of his paintings are on display at Tate St Ives.

Local legend It's interesting to speculate what DH Lawrence would have made of being a major protagonist in someone else's novel. He appeared in the late Helen Dunmore's fictional tale *Zennor in Darkness* which was set during World War I. It had the novelist and Frieda befriend a young artist called Clare as she comforted her shell-shocked cousin. The book won the 1994 McKitterick Prize for debut novels by writers over 40.

♿ **Accessibility**
Only suitable for wheelchairs and pushchairs in Zennor village

🐕 **Dogs**
On leads on path through Carnelloe Farm, 5 to 6. No stiles

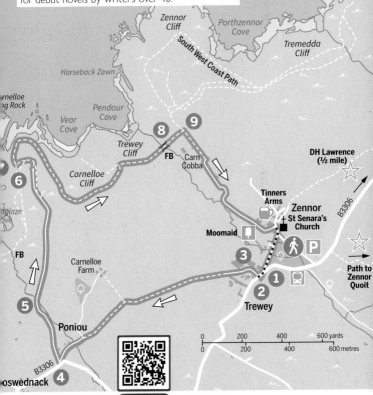

STORIES BEHIND THE WALK

☆ **Mermaid of Zennor chair** Inside St Senara's Church, you'll find a 400-year-old chair featuring an exquisitely carved mermaid. The story goes that there was a choirboy at St Senara's named Matthew Trewhella whose singing was so beautiful that it enchanted an equally melodious mermaid. They fell in love and she persuaded him to swim off with her. They were never seen again. The chair is believed to have been carved in memory of Matthew.

Zennor Quoit and DH Lawrence
(left, 1 mile)

☆ **DH Lawrence**
The renowned Nottinghamshire novelist fled with his German wife Frieda to Zennor's Higher Tregerthen farmhouse (just over 1 mile east of the village, off B3306) during World War I. They attempted to found a writers' commune – Katherine Mansfield and others came to stay – but the project was not a success. Suspected of spying and signalling to German U-boats from their house, the couple were ordered to leave the area or be arrested. Their stay was not entirely wasted though – Lawrence completed *Women in Love* there.

☆

🚶 ①②③

📱 B3306

🅿 Moomaid

Zennor car park

½ mile

➡ Leave the car park onto the village lane and turn **right**, heading up an incline to a road junction (B3306) at the top.

① ➡ Turn **right** at the T-junction and walk 50 yards to a turning on the right.

☆ Zennor Quoit

Consisting of seven upright stones and a partially collapsed double capstone, this colossal megalithic burial chamber lies on moorland 1 mile east of Zennor. Dating from around 4000 BP, it's the focus of a local legend: should its stones ever be removed, they'll magically reassemble themselves on the same spot. The capstone is estimated to weigh about 13.5 tons, so that would be quite a feat.

☆ John Davey

The Cornish language has had something of a resurgence in recent years and there are now dozens of courses available for those who wish to learn the Celtic tongue. It's a remarkable turnaround given that 1891 saw the death of Zennor resident John Davey, 'the last to possess any considerable Knowledge of the Cornish Language'. And even he wasn't fluent. He apparently ended up speaking Cornish with his cat (who in all likelihood wasn't fluent either).

4 B3306 (ahead)

5

⋮ 1 mile

▶ Go **right** onto a track past Trewey Barns and walk 50 yards to an open footpath gateway just in front of a farmyard.

3 ▶ Keep **straight ahead** across several small fields for about ½ mile until the path becomes a track, which leads on towards the B3306.

4 ▶ 20 yards before the road, turn **right** along a track to a gate in 300 yards.

NATURE NOTES

The jigsaw puzzle of tiny stone-walled irregular fields between Zennor and the sea is a reminder of a distant past when farming methods were very different to those practised today. On some of those walls you'll see pennywort, so called because its leaves are roughly the size and shape of an old penny. Also known as navelwort, in medieval times it was erroneously believed to have a cooling effect on the stomach and liver.

Other plants you'll see along the way include sea campion with its purple-veined calyx, greater plantain, recognisable by its straw-coloured flower spikes, wild roses, fuchsias, and an unlikely stand of bamboo planted just inside a gate as you head towards the sea at ⑤.

Along farmland hedgerows, listen and look out for yellowhammer and chaffinch, and on the coastal heathland keep your eyes peeled for common lizard, which move very quickly so that all you might see is a tail disappearing into the vegetation.

Left: pennywort
Above: wild rose
Right: fuchsia

White cottage

Dramatic stony outcrops

⑥

⑦

Tre
Pen

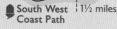

Carnelloe Cliff and Veor Cove

🚶 **South West Coast Path**   ⋮1½ miles

⑤ ➠ Go **right**, through the gate, and follow a grassy track for just over ⅓ mile towards a white cottage below.

⑥ ➠ Pass the cottage on a footpath to the **right** and follow it onwards as it bends left to reach the South West Coast Path.

⑦ ➠ At the coast path, by some dramatic stony outcrops, turn **right**, following a tiny handmade Zennor sign.
➠ The coast path leads you to a wooden footbridge in just over ½ mile.

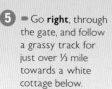  

Wind-sculpted holly

Chaffinch

Above: yellowhammer
Below: common lizard

St Senara's Church ⚑ 2½ miles

Carn Cobba

and ⑨

Tinners Arms (left) ☕

Zennor car park 🅿

Wooden footbridge

⑧

2 miles

Moomaid

⑧ ➡ **Cross** the bridge over a fast-flowing cliffside stream.
➡ Continue up steps on the far side towards a substantial house called Carn Cobba to reach a path T-junction at the top, to the left of the house.

⑨ ➡ Turn **right** at the junction.
➡ The path soon becomes a hard gravel track leading back to Zennor church. The car park is to your right, beyond the Tinners Arms.

WALK 6

CATCH A BUS

HELSTON

Stretching between Helston and the sea, the National Trust's Penrose Estate is wonderful for walkers. The smooth, wide, tarred track that runs from the entrance deep into the wooded park has also made it accessible to wheelchair users and pushchairs. Look out for the remnants of various arcane estate constructions along the way, as well as the impressive former gatehouse, Helston Lodge (now a National Trust holiday let), and fine views of The Loe.

OS information

🅰 SW 653270
Explorer 103

Distance
3.2 miles/5.1km

Time
2 hours

Start/Finish
Helston

Parking TR13 0RA
Fairground car park,
Porthleven Road

Public toilets
The Stables 🄳;
Helston

Cafés/pubs
Lakeside Café,
Coronation Park
(opposite 🅰); The
Stables 🄳; Helston

Terrain
Tarred track

Hilliness
Level throughout

Footwear
Year round 🥾

🚌 **Public transport**
Bus services 34
(Redruth and Lizard
via Helston) and
36 (Truro and St
Keverne via Helston)
with edge-of-town
bus stops at Tesco
and Sainsbury's:
gocornwallbus.co.uk

Did you know? A shipwreck off Loe Bar led to a change in the law. On 28 December 1807, Royal Navy frigate *HMS Anson* sank here. Between 60 and 190 men were lost (an unknown number of previously press-ganged survivors are believed to have deserted). The dead were buried in pits nearby without burial rites. This caused such a furore that the Burial of Drowned Persons Act was passed the following year.

Local legend The annual Hal-an-Tow is an integral part of the Furry Dance (see page 50). Performed by locals at various sites around Helston, it's a form of mystery play. However, rather than tell a Bible story, it relates the legends of Robin Hood, Friar Tuck, Saint George and others, while cocking a snook at raiding Spaniards. Sadly, its origins and even the meaning of its name are lost in the mists of time.

Scan Me

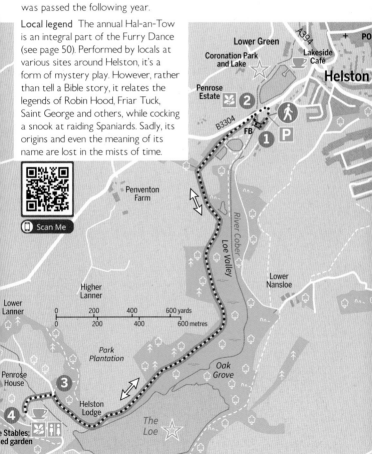

STORIES BEHIND THE WALK

🦋 **Penrose Estate** Named after the family that held land here for centuries, the 1,500-acre estate now belongs to the National Trust and includes not only The Loe (see opposite) but Loe Bar as well. The walled garden ❹ was designed by the Rev John Rogers in the 1770s when the estate was a vast 10,000-acre concern. A 17th-century country house on the estate remains in private hands, the current owner having inherited it by dint of a DNA test.

☆ **Coronation Park and Lake** (opposite)

☕ Lakeside Café

☆ **Furry Dance**
Made famous in the 1970s (as the *Floral Dance*) by both the Brighouse and Rastrick Brass Band and Terry Wogan, the Furry Dance is a folk pageant celebrating the coming of spring. Helston's version – usually held on 8 May – is the most famous and goes back to at least 1790. Local people take part in a series of dances throughout the town, wearing a sprig of lily of the valley.

L o e   V a l l e y

½ mile

P Fairground car park

Wooden footbridge

Penrose Estate

➡ In the first section of the car park, on the side nearest the road, look for and then cross a wooden footbridge.

♿ **Alternative wheelchair start in wet conditions**
➡ Near the car park entrance, leave by the Helston Hellys information board, going **left** for 100 yards along the pavement to a gate and Penrose Estate noticeboard and a tarred pathway.
➡ Read on from ❷.

☆ **The Loe** Covering 120 acres, this is Cornwall's biggest natural freshwater lake. It was established after the Loe Bar formed, cutting off the River Cober estuary from the Atlantic. There's uncertainty over when that happened (estimates range from 700 to several thousand years ago) and how it occurred (there are various competing theories and a fable that the giant Tregeagle dropped a bag of sand there) but it has undoubtedly created a special environment where rare plants and insects thrive.

Loe Valley

1 mile

Oak Grove

☆ **The Loe**
(left)

3

1½ miles

1 ➡ Bear **right** for 20 yards until you reach a Penrose Estate noticeboard on a tarred path by a gate.

2 ➡ Proceed along the tarred path for 1⅓ miles to a fingerpost and access drive junction, having kept **straight ahead** past the former gatehouse known as Helston Lodge 350 yards before the junction.

NATURE NOTES

Fears of flooding in Helston led to the straightening of the River Cober in the 1960s. Unfortunately, this had the effect of drying the natural wet woodland and it's only recently that conservation efforts have begun to restore this rare habitat. This has been great news for dragonflies, amphibians, small mammals, otters and birds. Visit in the evening and you may see bats flitting about or the ghost-like form of a barn owl.

Beech and holly both thrive here, while the ground beneath them is strewn with ferns and red campion. In the colder months of the year, stop a while to enjoy the view of The Loe near Helston Lodge

3 – close to 80 species of birds have been recorded overwintering on the lake, such as greenshank and long-tailed duck, while great crested grebe can be seen year round.

The margins of The Loe are a great place to observe damselflies, with the common blue and large red damselflies and the beautiful demoiselle three of the most common species. Damselflies rest with their wings closed, dragonflies with their wings open.

The Stables; walled garden

☆ T h e   L o e
(right)
Helston Lodge

Oak Grove

2 miles

☆ **Coronation Park and Lake**

After your walk, do cross the road from the car park entrance to visit Coronation Park and its large boating lake. The park opened in 1912, a year after the coronation of George V. It was conceived by borough surveyor William John Winn as somewhere purely and simply for the pleasure of the people of Helston (but visitors from elsewhere are welcome too). A wheelchair-friendly footpath/cycle track circumnavigates the lake.

Above: beautiful demoiselle
Below: large red damselfly

Top: greenshank
Above: beech trees
Opposite: long-tailed duck

Coronation Park and Lake (opposite) ☆

Lakeside Café

3 miles
2½ miles

Wooden footbridge

Penrose Estate

Fairground car park

3 ➡ At the fingerpost, turn **left** along a broad access drive signed to The Stables/Loe Bar/Porthleven via Coast to reach The Stables (National Trust).

4 ➡ After refreshment and a visit to the walled garden, return to the start by retracing your outward steps.

THE LIZARD

Its name derived from the Cornish 'lezou' meaning simply 'headland', the Lizard peninsula has a character all of its own. And the little village of Lizard, near the southern tip, provides a handy starting point for a clifftop adventure. The view from the coastal path at ⑥ of the sea crashing into the rocks in Housel Cove on a windy day can be wonderfully dramatic. Halfway round you can refresh yourself in a café perched high on Britain's most southerly point.

OS information

⊗ SW 703125
Explorer 103

Distance
2.7 miles/4.3km

Time
1¾ hours

Start/Finish
Lizard

Parking TR12 7NH
The Square car park

Public toilets
The Square, Lizard;
Lizard Lighthouse
car park

Cafés/pubs
Lizard village; Lizard
Point

Terrain
Pavement, lanes,
stony tracks and
grassy paths

Hilliness
Undulating

Footwear
Winter 🥾
Spring/Summer/
Autumn 👟

**Public
transport**
Bus stop by the car park. Bus service 34 (Redruth via Helston to Lizard): gocornwallbus. co.uk; the Lizard service from Helston: firstbus.co.uk

Did you know? It was on Lizard Point that the first sighting of the Spanish Armada was made on the afternoon of 19 July 1588. News of the invasion force was swiftly transmitted from The Lizard to London, 250 miles away, by a series of beacons built along the south coast.

Local legend The story of the 200-odd victims from the *Royal Anne* disaster (see page 56) being buried in unconsecrated pits in Pistil Meadow is a grim one indeed. The sad tale was re-told by novelists Wilkie Collins and Daphne du Maurier, and is still cited by apparently reliable sources today. However, investigations in 2016 by the Maritime Archaeology Sea Trust uncovered no geophysical evidence for it at all. The mystery now is why such a legend began.

♿ **Accessibility**
▪▪▪▪▪▪▪▪▪▪▪
Wheelchairs and pushchairs around Lizard village ⓚ to ❷, and ❾ to end. Disabled parking and access at Lizard Point

🐕 **Dogs**
Welcome but keep on leads in village and where there are livestock near Lizard Point. No stiles

STORIES BEHIND
THE WALK

☆ **Most southerly point** The British mainland's most southerly tip is a finger of land overlooking the dangerous rocks of Vellan Drang, with Polpeor and Polbream coves on either side. A few shed-like buildings are perched precariously along its length, defying the elements. Remarkably, two of those buildings – the café and gift shop – seem impervious to everything that the Atlantic throws at them. They look almost exactly the same today as in picture postcard photos taken 70 years ago.

☆ **Shipwrecks** With its sharp rocks jutting out into the Atlantic, Lizard Point has accounted for a vast quantity of shipping. With a tempest raging about them, many a frightened sailor and passenger has attempted to make their soul right with God. One such storm in November 1721 drove the galley frigate *Royal Anne* into the rocks en route to Barbados. From the ship's complement of around 200 there were just three survivors.

The Lizard Chapel ✚

Beacon Terrace

The Square car park

① Moyleroe (last house on the right)

② Long barn (50 yards ahead)

③

④ ½ mile

⑤

Hous Cov ⑥

➡ Leave the Square by following the Church Cove fingerpost sign across the road and along Beacon Terrace.

➡ Pass a park and field (right) to reach a junction.

① ➡ Turn **right** down Housel Bay Road for 150 yards, passing The Lizard Chapel, to Moyleroe, the last house on the right.

☆ Lizard Lighthouse

It was on account of the dangers involved in passing Lizard Point that a tower with a light on it was built in 1619. However, it proved too expensive to maintain and was demolished 11 years later. Today's lighthouse was constructed in 1751 by merchant and politician Thomas Fonnereau. Unusually, it had two towers, each topped by a coal-burning brazier. Nowadays, the lighthouse is electrified, automated, uses just one tower and houses its own heritage centre (trinityhouse.co.uk).

☆ Old lifeboat station

Look down the cliffs just after passing the café and you'll see a large shed with a ramp. This is the old lifeboat station which operated from 1859 to 1961. Its location meant that the busy station was exposed to the vicissitudes of the sea, making any launch in stormy weather a perilous activity. The station was thus closed and a new one built a few miles round the coast at the more sheltered Kilcobben Cove.

Lizard Lighthouse ☆

Most southerly point; old lifeboat station; shipwrecks

South West Coast Path

1 mile

Polbream Cove

☆

7

Wavecrest Café

2 ▸ Immediately after the house, turn **right** through a five-bar gate into a field.
▸ After 30 yards, go through a metal gate and continue **ahead**, aiming for a long barn on the far side.

3 ▸ About 50 yards before the barn, turn **left** to follow a fence along the field edge towards the sea to reach a gateway at the bottom of the field.

4 ▸ Pass through the gateway into a smaller field.
▸ Head down to a kissing-gate in the bottom right-hand corner.

NATURE NOTES

Having vanished from Cornwall (and England) in 1973 following a long decline in numbers, a few choughs unexpectedly returned to the county in 2001. Though still a very rare site nationally, they have built up a small stronghold on Lizard Point. Featuring on the Cornish coat of arms, choughs resemble small crows but with red legs and bills. If you're lucky, you may also get to see a kestrel hovering above the clifftops, carefully spying the grassland for a tasty small rodent.

The cliffs above Polpeor and Polbream coves are carpeted with hottentot figs. An invasive species from South Africa, it can also be seen in great quantities on the Isles of Scilly. Sadly, it's pushing out native plants such as the rare prostrate asparagus. Look out for twin-headed clover, another rarity, alongside more common wildflowers such as speedwell.

Watch, too, for grey seals – you may see one bobbing in the sea in Polpeor Cove – and even basking sharks, as there are regular sightings along the Cornish coast during the summer.

The clouded yellow is a migratory butterfly, crossing the English Channel to breed on the warm, south-facing slopes of The Lizard. Their caterpillars feed on clover and the butterflies can usually be seen from June until October.

South West Coast Path

Pistil Meadow   Lizard Point   Venton Hill Point   2 miles

1½ miles

Lizard Point car park (right, 250 yards)

5 ➡ Go through the kissing-gate and after 15 yards turn **left** along a footpath between hedges.
➡ After 125 yards, meet the South West Coast Path joining from the left.

6 ➡ Keep **forward** onto the coast path, following the waymarker: Lizard Point ¾ mile.
➡ Keep along the coast path to a footbridge and up onto the clifftops above Housel Cove and onwards, past the lighthouse, to the most southerly point.

7 ➡ Continue along the coast path to the **left** of Wavecrest Café.
➡ Enter Pistil Meadow in 275 yards, and ignore footpaths inland until, ⅓ mile after rounding Lizard Point, you reach a grassy path above Crane Ledges/ Holseer Cove.

Above: chough
Below: kestrel

Top: clouded yellow butterfly
Bottom: hottentot fig

L i z a r d H e a d L a n e

9

2½ miles
The Square car park

Holseer Cove;
Crane Ledges

8 ➽ Turn **right**, almost back on yourself, on a grassy path leading to a gate 125 yards away.
➽ Pass through the gate and head on up a track between walls (Lizard Head Lane), coming to a T-junction in ½ mile.

9 ➽ At the junction, turn **left** to pass along a track in front of houses.
➽ The track becomes a metalled road leading back to The Square.

Walk 7 The Lizard **59**

Opposite (clockwise):
Polpeor Café, The Lizard;
Tinners Arms, Zennor
This page (clockwise):
Olive Tree, Bude; King
Arthur's Arms, Tintagel;
The Moomaid of Zennor;
The Bullfrog, St Agnes;
The Heligan Takeaway,
Lost Gardens of Heligan

Tinners Arms

61

WALK 8

TRELISSICK

Set on its own small peninsula on the west bank of the wide River Fal, Trelissick feels like a little world unto itself. The estate was given to the National Trust in 1955 and this walk explores the beautiful mixed woodland on both sides of the Lamouth Creek. It also takes a tour around Iron Age Roundwood Fort, passes the King Harry Ferry and affords many a ravishing view through the trees and over the Fal.

OS information	
🧭 SW 835396 Explorer 105	
Distance 3.1 miles/5km	
Time 2 hours	
Start/Finish Trelissick	
Parking TR3 6QL Trelissick National Trust car park	
Public toilets Trelissick	
Cafés/pubs Crofters Café, Trelissick	
Terrain Woodland and grassy paths; stony tracks; lanes	
Hilliness One descent ❷ to ❸; one long but gentle ascent ❼ to end	
Footwear Winter 🥾 Spring/Summer/Autumn 👟	
🚌 **Public transport** Bus service 493, Truro circular: travelcornwall.uk.com; King Harry Ferry: falriver.co.uk/ferries/king-harry-ferry	

Did you know? On the far bank of the Fal sits lonely Tolverne (or Smugglers) Cottage. A Grade II-listed thatched residence built of slate stone rubble in the 1600s, it's a vision of tranquillity and a distant bucolic past. It's hard to believe that this was the spot where thousands of American troops embarked to take part in the D-Day Landings. General Eisenhower himself stayed in the cottage during the preparations.

Local legends Trelissick House was long rumoured to have a secret tunnel. In this case, the rumours turned out to be true. One end of it can now be seen from the cellars. However, since it has yet to be explored, its destination is still cloaked in mystery. There's a secret garden near the house so it's possible it has a hidden exit there. Though who dug it and why are questions that still hang tantalizingly in the air.

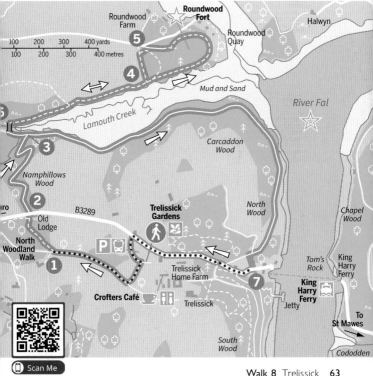

STORIES BEHIND
THE WALK

Trelissick Gardens With the house having changed hands at least ten times since it was built in the 1750s, the gardens at Trelissick have seen many changes over the centuries. However, what has remained a constant is the mild marine micro-climate that allows for the cultivation of exotic plants. Look out too for the wonderful Japanese red cedar planted in 1898, and an orchard planted this century to preserve local apple varieties.

☆ **River Fal** One of Britain's most picturesque rivers, the Fal rises on Goss Moor and flows out to sea at Falmouth. It's a typical ria: a river valley flooded by rising seas at the end of the last Ice Age. It's also a fair indicator of how much trade is being done globally – when there's a downturn you'll see plenty of cargo ships mothballed in the upper estuary awaiting busier times.

2 Old Lodge

Namphillows Wood

1 North Woodland Walk sign

½ mile

Footbridge **3**

National Trust car park
Crofters Café

➥ Leave the NT car park by the attendant's shelter, heading for a metal gate.
➥ Through the gate, follow the path briefly to a T-junction and turn **right** along a hard gravel track for 300 yards to a cattle grid.

1 ➥ Just beyond the cattle grid, turn **right** up a woodland path signed North Woodland Walk.
➥ Walk through woodland to the Old Lodge in 175 yards.

☆ Roundwood Fort

Roundwood Fort's contours and ridges are nowadays mostly disguised by the attractive mixed woodland that covers it. However, with a little detective work it is still possible to make out the layout of the place. In the Iron Age it was an important defensive position and a rare one at that because very few overlooked estuaries. Two high ramparts once blocked off the end of the promontory, helping to safeguard the round enclosure.

🖼 King Harry Ferry

Since it chops a full 26 miles off the road journey from one side to the other of the River Fal, it's no surprise that there's been a ferry crossing here since at least the Middle Ages. It probably takes its name from a long-ruined chapel on the eastern side that was dedicated to St Mary and King Henry VI. Though vehicles are charged for this chain-ferry crossing, pedestrians are merely asked to give a donation to charity.

Lamouth Creek   Fort plaque on boulder   **Roundwood Fort** (left) ☆   Optional path to Roundwood Quay (right)   **5**   Fort plaque on boulder

4   1 mile   1½ miles

2 ➡ At the Old Lodge, go through the gate, cross the road with care, pass through a gate on the far side, and head downhill through woodland on a zigzagging path to a T-junction in 500 yards.

3 ➡ At the T-junction, turn **left** towards a wooden footbridge below.
➡ After 40 yards, turn **right** to reach and cross the bridge.
➡ Continue with Lamouth Creek on your right for ⅓ mile to a National Trust plaque signed Roundwood Fort.

NATURE NOTES

The woods at Trelissick comprise a wide variety of deciduous trees that give interest to the walk all year round. However, they're particularly inspiring in spring when the bright green of young leaves gives them a joyous fresh look, and in autumn when the russets and golds predominate. There are mighty birch trees to enjoy, along with limes and oaks. And in October you'll find the sweet chestnuts bristling with their prickly cased fruit.

Fungi love woodland, particularly where tree stumps and fallen branches are left to rot. Orange pore fungus is no exception and can be seen growing alongside the trail, readily identified by its vivid orange spores. Rhinoceros beetles also live in and around dead wood, and the males have a distinctive horn-like protuberance on their heads.

And don't forget to look up too. Buzzards patrol Trelissick's skies and sparrowhawks are apex predators in the woodland.

Oak

Footbridge
6

2 miles

C a r c a

L a m o u t h   C r e e k

4 ➡ At plaque, note path on left for the return; for now, keep **ahead**.
➡ After the path has curved left, an optional turn right leads to steps down to Roundwood Quay, an excellent picnic spot.
➡ Otherwise, continue looping round the fort to a five-bar gate.

5 ➡ Through the gate, head **left** beside a lane, very soon bearing **left** again at a stone pillar.
➡ After 10 yards, turn **left** down a grassy path.
➡ At the bottom, by the plaque 4, turn **right** to return to the footbridge.

Top left: sparrowhawk
Above: acorns
Left: rhinoceros beetle
Below: sweet chestnut

North Wood
☆ R i v e r   F a l
W o o d
North Wood

3 miles

🛈 📅

🚲 King Harry Ferry   Trelissick Gardens
(left)

Crofters Café;
National Trust
car park

2½ miles

6 ➤ Over the bridge, turn **left** at a T-junction then keep **ahead** to follow the other (south) bank of Lamouth Creek and the western shore of the River Fal for 1 mile, eventually descending steps to emerge by King Harry Ferry.

7 ➤ Turn **right** up the road to return to the car park.
➤ For a shortcut to visit the gardens, cross the road by the ferry terminal and climb the steps. The entrance is to your right.

LOST GARDENS
OF HELIGAN

The story of the Lost Gardens of Heligan (see page 70) is one of terrible sadness and inspiring renewal. The gardens are a pleasant stroll up from the pretty little port of Mevagissey, whose credentials as a fishing village are cemented by the fact that its streetlights were once powered by oil extracted from pilchards. You can enjoy the wonderful flora on show at Heligan by taking this almost entirely off-road route up from Mevagissey on a shared path that is suitable for wheelchairs.

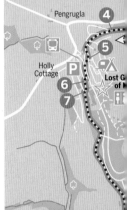

OS information

⊗ SX 012451
Explorer 105

Distance
3.9 miles/6.2km

Time
2½ hours

Start/Finish
Mevagissey

Parking PL26 6SB
Willow car and coach park, Valley Road

Public toilets
Lost Gardens of Heligan; Valley Road, Mevagissey (100 yards south of car park)

Cafés/pubs
Lost Gardens of Heligan; Mevagissey

Terrain
Generally smooth, hard-surfaced tracks and pavement

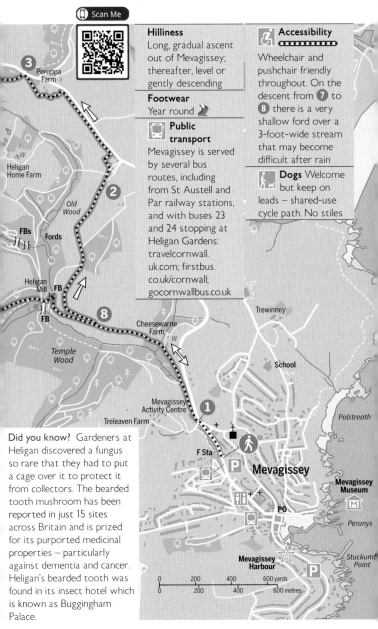

Scan Me

Hilliness
Long, gradual ascent out of Mevagissey; thereafter, level or gently descending

Footwear
Year round

Public transport
Mevagissey is served by several bus routes, including from St Austell and Par railway stations, and with buses 23 and 24 stopping at Heligan Gardens: travelcornwall. uk.com; firstbus. co.uk/cornwall; gocornwallbus.co.uk

Accessibility
Wheelchair and pushchair friendly throughout. On the descent from ⑦ to ⑧ there is a very shallow ford over a 3-foot-wide stream that may become difficult after rain

Dogs Welcome but keep on leads – shared-use cycle path. No stiles

Did you know? Gardeners at Heligan discovered a fungus so rare that they had to put a cage over it to protect it from collectors. The bearded tooth mushroom has been reported in just 15 sites across Britain and is prized for its purported medicinal properties – particularly against dementia and cancer. Heligan's bearded tooth was found in its insect hotel which is known as Buggingham Palace.

Peruppa Farm

Heligan Home Farm

Old Wood

FBs   Fords

Heligan Mill   FB

FB

Temple Wood

Cheesewarne Farm

Trewinney

School

Mevagissey Activity Centre

Treleaven Farm

F Sta

Mevagissey

Polstreath

Mevagissey Museum

PO

Perunys

Mevagissey Harbour

Stuckumb Point

0   200   400   600 yards
0   200   400   600 metres

STORIES BEHIND
THE WALK

☆ **Lost Gardens of Heligan** The 1,000-acre
Heligan estate was an unlikely victim of World War I.
The extraordinary gardens there were tended by a
phalanx of gardeners, many of whom went over to
France never to return. Heligan was then 'lost to the
brambles of time' as the current owners poetically put
it. It was rediscovered in 1990 and became the largest
garden restoration project in Europe, now offering
visitors 200 glorious acres in which to ramble
(heligan.com).

Potting Shed

☆ **Mevagissey Harbour** Back in the
Middle Ages, Mevagissey had a mere quay where
its fine harbour sits now. Or rather, where its
harbours sit, because the original 18th-century
one was supplemented by an outer harbour
in 1888 as Mevagissey's fishing fleet grew in
size. At that time no fewer than 60 fishing
boats plied the waters for mackerel, herring
and pilchard. The harbour remains a busy place
today, giving haven to fishing vessels and day-
tripper boats.

Mevagissey
Activity Centre

Cheeswarne Farm

½ mile

Willow
car and
coach
park

➡ Leave the car park by the
vehicle exit in the top corner,
cross the road carefully and
turn **right**.
➡ Walk 300 yards to
Mevagissey Activity Centre.

1 ➡ At the centre, bear **left** along
a wide surfaced cycle/footpath
signed Heligan.
➡ Follow this for 1 mile, ignoring
paths off to the left, to reach a
Coastal & Clay Trail three-way
fingerpost.

Mevagissey Museum The building that houses Mevagissey's museum is a vital piece of the town's history itself. Built in 1745 directly into the rock face, it was a boat builders' yard right up until the last shipwright retired and offered to sell it to the museum. The story of Mevagissey over the centuries is brought to life by exhibits such as a horse-drawn barley thresher and a Cornish kitchen, and a host of fascinating old photographs and artefacts (mevagisseymuseum.com).

☆ **Feast Week** While places like Helston organise their own annual day of festivities (see page 50), Mevagissey revels in a whole week. Celebrated since the Middle Ages, for centuries it was a December occasion. However, since adopting the fisherman St Peter in the 1750s, it's been held around his feast day of 29 June. Entertainments include exhibitions, parades and floral dances, fish dishes, choirs and bands, children's competitions, raft races, a fête and a firework display (mevagisseyfeastweek.org.uk).

mile   2   1½ miles   Peruppa Farm   3

2 ➡ Turn **left**, signed Heligan Gardens and Pentewan.
➡ Stay on this metalled path for ½ mile to reach a T-junction and another three-way fingerpost.

3 ➡ At the T-junction, turn **left** along a crushed stone track signed Heligan Gardens.
➡ Follow the track for ¼ mile to a Tremayne Estates notice on the edge of a campsite.

4 ➡ Keep **straight ahead** on a permissive path through the Heligan campsite for 200 yards or so to reach a Heligan Gardens sign.

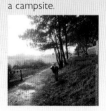

NATURE NOTES

Douglas fir

The Jungle at Heligan plays host to some of the more unusual plants to be introduced to Britain. Towering tree ferns hail from far-away New Zealand while banana plants also thrive in the subtropical gardens. At the entrance to the Northern Gardens a venerable Douglas fir demands attention. It has a rare genetic mutation that has given rise to a flourishing witch's broom – a dense mass of shoots from a single point.

On your way up to Heligan, keep a look out for the sheep in the fields beside the path. You should be able to spot the well-named badger face Welsh mountain sheep grazing alongside handsome Jacob sheep, recognisable by their ink-blot patterned wool and fine curved horns. In many places the sides of the path are garlanded with the delicate small mauve flowers of herb Robert.

In the summer, boat trips operate out of Mevagissey harbour to watch marine wildlife and seabirds, typically seeking to spot: Atlantic bluefin tuna, common and bottlenose dolphin, basking shark and leatherback turtle (outtheblueboatcharters.co.uk).

Lost Gardens
of Heligan
☆

2 miles

2½ miles

Heligan Caravan
and Camping Park

5 ➤ Turn **right**, in the direction of the sign.
➤ Almost immediately go through a gate, cross a road, pass through another gate and turn **left** to head through a car park.

6 ➤ At the car park's end, on the right, pass between a lone beech and a Lost Gardens of Heligan sign.
➤ To visit the gardens, carry on **ahead** through the arches to the café, takeaway, shop and entrance. Otherwise, turn **right**.

7 ➤ Immediately go **left** along a wide track.
➤ Follow this for 1 mile, keeping **right** just after Butler's Cottage, to meet the cycle/footpath used on the outward leg.

The Jungle at Heligan

Above: Jacob sheep
Middle: herb Robert
Bottom: bluefin tuna

Mevagissey Harbour and
Museum (ahead, ⅓ mile)

Heligan Mill ┊ 3 miles ── 8 ── Cheesewarne Farm ┊ 3½ miles ── Willow car and coach park ⛪ 🅼

🅟

3 ■ Turn **right** to retrace your steps for ⅔ mile to return to the start.

Local legend Mevagissey's 400-year-old Ship Inn is the site of a pleasingly gentle tale of mild intrigue. When the photograph of the late Lil Barron – a former landlady – went missing from behind the bar in 2012, the owners reported that the pub suddenly became prone to frequent flooding. Eventually, the photograph was discovered and returned, and the flooding mysteriously stopped.

MOUNT EDGCUMBE

Cornish people often speak of 'going up to England' if they head into Devon. Going the other way – from England into Cornwall on Plymouth's Cremyll Ferry – is undoubtedly the most pleasurable means of arriving at Mount Edgcumbe. There's so much to see and do in this 500-acre former estate that you can spend a whole day here. This circular walk takes in many of the highlights, including the house, the National Camellia Collection, Milton's Temple, the formal gardens and two excellent cafés (mountedgcumbe.gov.uk).

OS information

🚶 SX 452532
Explorer 108

Distance
2.2 miles/3.6 km

Time
1½ hours

Start/Finish
Mount Edgcumbe Cremyll Ferry Gate

Parking PL1 3RL, Strand Street car park, Plymouth (for the Cremyll Ferry); PL10 1HU, Cremyll car park

Public toilets
The Barrow Centre (accessible by wheelchair-friendly lift); next to The Orangery

Cafés/pubs
The Farriers café at the Barrow Centre, and The Orangery; Edgcumbe Arms, Cremyll

Terrain
Stone and surfaced tracks

Hilliness
One ascent to Mount Edgcumbe House ❶ to ❷, one descent ❻ to ❼

Footwear
Year round 👢

Did you know? The Bath chair was actually invented in Bath (though its name may come from its bath-like appearance). This walk takes you past a Victorian Bath chair that belonged to Lady Katherine, 4th Countess of Mount Edgcumbe. Designed to be pulled by human or beast, it tells a sad story. A devoted mother of four, Lady Katherine used it because she suffered from consumption (tuberculosis). She died in 1874 aged just 34.

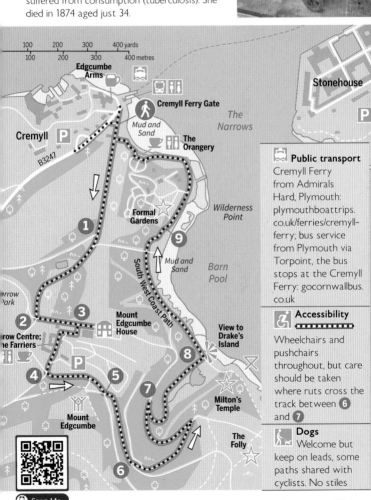

Public transport
Cremyll Ferry from Admirals Hard, Plymouth: plymouthboattrips.co.uk/ferries/cremyll-ferry; bus service from Plymouth via Torpoint, the bus stops at the Cremyll Ferry: gocornwallbus.co.uk

Accessibility
Wheelchairs and pushchairs throughout, but care should be taken where ruts cross the track between 6 and 7

Dogs
Welcome but keep on leads, some paths shared with cyclists. No stiles

STORIES BEHIND
THE WALK

Mount Edgcumbe House Built between 1547 and 1550 for Sir Richard Edgcumbe, the house was once rather larger than today. On the night of 21 March 1941, Plymouth was bombed by the Luftwaffe. An incendiary device fell on the building, setting it alight and destroying it. The 6th Earl of Mount Edgcumbe and his wife Lilian spent six years and a colossal sum reconstructing what they could of the house, both dying shortly after the work was completed.

☆ **The Folly** Up on the hillside towards the eastern end of the park stands a ruined stone tower. A fragment of a castle, perhaps? The remains of a lookout tower? No, it's merely a folly, built in 1747 (though it does unwittingly also serve as a navigation aid). However, were you to mistake it for the remnants of some sacred building you wouldn't be far wrong – it's constructed from materials taken from two local churches, St George's and St Lawrence's.

Mount Edgcumbe Cremyll Ferry Gate
- Arriving by ferry/bus, the entrance gate is 100 yards **left** of ferry landing.
- Arriving by car, turn **left** out of car park along road and in 125 yards swing **right** to entrance.

(ahead, 100 yards)

Mount Edgcumbe Country Park

2
1 ½ mil

1

P Cremyll Ferry car park

Cremyll Ferry Gate

➡ Begin from Mount Edgcumbe's Cremyll Ferry Gate entrance.
➡ Keep **ahead** on a tree-lined path for 300 yards to a junction.

1 ➡ Where the track divides, continue **forward** and follow it rising gently with Mount Edgcumbe House up ahead to a fingerpost and T-junction.

☆ Gardens at Edgcumbe

Covering around 100 acres, Mount Edgcumbe's pleasure grounds are a treasure trove for historians. Expanded by succeeding generations of wealthy Edgcumbes from the 16th century onwards, they include seven acres of formal gardens. There's truly something for everyone. The Italian Garden, French Garden, American Garden, English Garden, Fern Dell, New Zealand Garden and Rose Garden are just a selection of the horticultural delights on offer.

☆ Drake's Island

Previously known as St Michael and then St Nicolas, the island came under the governorship of Sir Francis Drake in 1583. Over the centuries it has served as a fort, a prison, a pilgrimage destination, an observatory and, more recently, a youth adventure centre. Furthermore, the world's earliest recorded submarine fatality occurred off its shores in 1774. The current owner intends to install a heritage centre and open the isle to the public.

Mount Edgcumbe House

National Camellia Collection

The Farriers, Barrow Centre

1 mile

2 ➡ Turn **left** to visit or simply admire Edgcumbe House.
➡ Then turn **back** the way you came a short distance to a Barrow Centre signpost.

3 ➡ Turn **left** for the Barrow Centre.
➡ Continue up the pathway past the courtyard café and, shortly afterwards, reach a fingerpost marked Cawsand.

4 ➡ Go **left** in the Cawsand direction.
➡ Where the track divides, continue **forwards**, following another Cawsand sign.
➡ Keep **ahead** for 150 yards to next fingerpost and junction.

NATURE NOTES

Starting with just 70 plants in 1976, Mount Edgcumbe's National Camellia Collection now contains over a thousand different varieties and species. The plants' dainty flowers begin to appear from January onwards, bringing a welcome splash of colour to winter. On the Camellia Trail you'll see a wide selection, including two fine varieties of *Camellia sasanqua* – Hugh Evans and Paradise Glow.

The park's woods play host to a wide variety of flora, including colourful maples and distinctive large-leafed gunnera that looks like giant rhubarb.

A visit to the formal gardens is not complete without passing through the Jubilee Garden with its sculptural topiary, and the Rose Garden, with a collection of David Austin Old English roses.

In 2017, England's first black bee reserve was established in the formal gardens. Deeper into the country park there is a herd of wild fallow deer.

Jubilee Garden

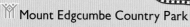

☆ **The Folly** (250 yards, right)

pond; Milton's Temple (right)

View to Drake's Islan

Mount Edgcumbe Country Park   1½ miles

South West Coast Path

5 ▸ Turn **left** towards The Folly/Earls Drive and stroll to another fork in about 400 yards.
▸ This section is through the park's National Camellia Collection.

6 ▸ Go **left**, downhill.
▸ Ignore the first path off left but turn sharply **left** at the next.
▸ Stay with the Camellia Trail for 250 yards to a T-junction.

7 ▸ Turn sharp **right** on a wide concrete track to continue descending.
▸ At the bottom, pass a pond and Milton's Temple (right) and meet the sea at a picnic area.

Top left: *Camellia sasanqua*
Top right: gunnera
Above: black bee hives
Left: maple

☆ **Formal Gardens**   The Orangery   Cremyll Ferry Gate

Cremyll Ferry car park

2 miles

(ahead, 100 yards)

8 ➡ Turn **left** to walk alongside the shore of The Sound, joining the South West Coast Path.
➡ There are good views to Drake's Island across The Sound.
➡ Keep parallel with the shore to reach the Formal Gardens entrance.

9 ➡ Enter the Formal Gardens.
➡ Staying close by the shore, the path passes the entrance to The Orangery and leads back to the park's Cremyll Ferry Gate.

Publishing information

© Crown copyright 2023.
All rights reserved.

Ordnance Survey, OS, and the OS logos are registered trademarks, and OS Short Walks Made Easy is a trademark of Ordnance Survey Ltd.

© Crown copyright and database rights (2023) Ordnance Survey.

ISBN 978 0 319092 67 5
1st edition published by Ordnance Survey 2023.

www.ordnancesurvey.co.uk

While every care has been taken to ensure the accuracy of the route directions, the publishers cannot accept responsibility for errors or omissions, or for changes in details given. The countryside is not static: hedges and fences can be removed, stiles can be replaced by gates, field boundaries can alter, footpaths can be rerouted and changes in ownership can result in the closure or diversion of some concessionary paths. Also, paths that are easy and pleasant for walking in fine conditions may become slippery, muddy and difficult in wet weather.

If you find an inaccuracy in either the text or maps, please contact Ordnance Survey at os.uk/contact.

A catalogue record for this book is available from the British Library.

Milestone Publishing credits

Author: Dixe Wills

Series editor: Kevin Freeborn

Maps: Cosmographics

Design and Production: Patrick Dawson, Milestone Publishing

Printed in India by Replika Press Pvt. Ltd

Photography credits

Front cover: ClimbWhenReady/Shutterstock.com.
Back cover cornfield/Shutterstock.com.

All photographs supplied by the author ©Dixe Wills except page 6 Fi Darby; pages 38, 39 Kevin Freeborn; page 71 Nilfanion, CC BY-SA 4.0, via Wikimedia Commons.

The following images were supplied by Shutterstock.com: 5, 74 4 season backpacking; 47 AlekseyKarpenko; 47, 59 Alex Cooper Photography; 40 Anton Mizik; 25 Barbarajo; 53 Barry and Carole Bowden; 23, 70 chrisdorney; 30, 56 Clare Louise Jackson; 16 cornishpiglet; 67 Dan74; 25 David Havel; 59 Davide Bonora; 4, 48 diagon_sally; 19 Elena Terletskaya; 47 Giedriius; 26 Helen Hotson; 53 Henri_Lehtola; 3, 9, 13, 34, 52, ian woolcock; 67 IanRedding; 23 Irene Rios Photography; 17 J M Ritchie; 53 Jaco Visser; 7 jaroslava V; 52 Jim Nelson; 67 kacege; 67 Lillian Tveit; 73 Lorna Roberts; 72 Markus Stappen; 40, 56 Martin Fowler; 40 Neil Clarke; 73 Nicole Kwiatkowski; 41 Paolo Trovo; 27, 64 Paul Nash; 22 Peter Turner Photography; 73 Petra Hatrikova; 77, 79 RogerMechan; 31 Scorsby; 25 seeing in light; 19 Silva Vaughan-Jones; 41 Simon Burt; 33 snapvision; 5, 62 Stephen G Roberts; 1 Steve Meese; 19 stocktech78; 59 Szymon Bartosz; 57 Tom Meaker; 51 tony mills; 3, 20 Vivvi Smak.